CAMPUS MINISTRY

CAMPUS MINISTRY

HOW TO REACH YOUR CAMPUS FOR CHRIST

Roy S. Isbell, Sr.

AuthorHouse™
1663 Liberty Drive
Bloomington, IN 47403
www.authorhouse.com
Phone: 1-800-839-8640

First published by AuthorHouse 08/22/2011

ISBN: 978-1-4634-1957-8 (sc)
ISBN: 978-1-4634-1956-1 (hc)
ISBN: 978-1-4634-1955-4 (ebk)

Library of Congress Control Number: 2011910324

Printed in the United States of America

This book is printed on acid-free paper.

AUTHOR: ROY S. ISBELL

Forty-five years in college and university Campus Ministry activities.

Auburn University	1939-1941
Active in BSU & called to be a Campus Minister.	
Joined Navy as a pilot cadet WW II	1941-1945
Ordained to the ministry	1946
Southern Baptist Theological Seminary	1945-1948
Southwestern Baptist Seminary	1960-1961
Masters in Religious Education	
Campus Minister at Delta State University	1950-1951
Campus Minister at Mississippi State Univ	1951-1960
Campus Minister at University of Missouri	1961-1970
Associate Minister First Baptist Church Columbia, Missouri	1970-1974
Church Planter and Pastor of Midway Heights Baptist Church Columbia, Missouri	1975-1979
Home Mission Worker (College Ministry) Univ. of Mass. & North East New England, and Miami, Florida	1985-1991
Campus Minister at Florida Central University	1991-1992

Volunteer Campus Minister FL Atlantic Univ. 1994-1995

Author's Publishing History

Monthly BSU Newspaper for all Baptists 1953-1960 at Mississippi State University

Sunday School Lessons for the Missouri Baptist State Paper (Weekly) 1 Year

Radio Program "Spirit of BSU," Mississippi State University

THIS BOOK IS DEDICATED TO:

The Lord Jesus Christ the Son of the Living God who has inspired me to write so others may know Him and tell others about His saving Grace.

I am also dedicating this book and my Fatherly Blessings to my two children. Rev. R. Sherman Isbell, Jr. and Dr. Sally Powers, the wonderful mother of my two grandchildren. My granddaughter, Sophia Powers, accepted Jesus as her Lord and Savior with the leadership of the Holy Spirit and her Grandmother Lou Isbell. Max Powers, my grandson, is my pride and joy and I feel sure God has some great things for him to do and be.

TABLE OF CONTENTS

Roy and Lou Isbell (1946-1996)

To________
I pray this book will help you to know Jesus so
you can make Him known to others.
Your friend in Christ, Roy S. Isbell, Sr.

Preface

After 45 years of campus ministry service and the thrill of seeing college students accept Christ as their Lord and Savior and develop into outstanding leaders for Christ, I now have the opportunity to write about the rich spiritual experiences I have had with the Lord and other campus ministers.

The goal and Biblical command for campus ministry is to make disciples and to develop Christian leaders who know Jesus Christ as Lord of their life and are able to make Him known to others. My prayers and dreams for this book are to inspire, inform, and challenge others to develop a passionate, organized Christian witness on every college and university campus for the glory of God.

I want to thank my wife Ruth for her devotion, prayers and helpful suggestions in writing this book. I also want to thank her daughter Brenda Jones for help in formatting, and my daughter Dr. Sally Powers for putting the finishing touches to my writing. I want to thank the pastors who worked with me in my ministry: Dr. Charles Treadway in

Cleveland, Mississippi; D. C. Applegate in Starkville, Mississippi; Webster Brown, Roger Barnard, and Loy Reed in Columbia, Missouri; Truman Herring and Sandy Huntsman in Boca Raton, Florida; and Chris Crain, Michael Ethridge and Richard Hitchcock in Birmingham, Alabama.

CAMPUS MINISTRY

Introduction

This book will help you to develop a successful college ministry. It tells you how to get started and how to effectively organize a ministry. This book will inspire you to be creative in ministering to college students, whether they are single, married, or international, as well as to faculty and staff. Pastors and religious leaders who work with college students can use this book as their manual. It gives them the Biblical reasons and methods for reaching and ministering to the needs, desires, and bonding friendships of college students, faculty, and staff.

This book was inspired by God. As I was having my daily devotions, God laid the thought on my heart for me to write a book about my 45 years of experiences in student campus work. As I started writing, the Holy Spirit led me to the topics and content that should be included. I have experienced true joy of the Lord, as we worked together on this book.

This book tells you about God's mission field, and how God is bringing the mission field to our colleges and universities so that we may witness to the future leaders of the world. This program will meet the basic needs that students have of salvation, vocation, choosing a mate, Christian fellowship, and purpose in life. The ideas outlined in this book are part of a program that is supported by thousands of churches, for campus ministry is the church reaching out to the campus during the week. Christ's Church is reaching out in all directions to build a better world until Jesus comes to make all things new on earth as it is in Heaven.

Jerry Carmichael, director of Missouri BSU Ministries, asks if you can think of any other time in your life when more major life decisions were made, or beliefs and values embraced than those few tumultuous college years? College students stream through the doors of our ministry's building year after year, and we have the opportunity and mandate to shape and mold their young formative lives in the pursuit of Christ.

HOW TO REACH YOUR CAMPUS FOR CHRIST

Jesus Christ has given us the gift of salvation to share with the most important group of people, college students, in the most important time in their lives. In the next four or five years they will be making five of the most important decisions of their lives, if they have not already made them.

The first and most important decision is the student's personal relationship with Jesus Christ. Second is his or her choice of a mate to marry and spend the rest of life with. Third, students will choose their first vocation, and prepare to invest their life in that service. Fourth, they will be choosing their relationships with class members, faculty members, church members, sports, and social friends. Fifth, when they get married they need to decide what type of parent they want to be. Do they love children? How will they prepare to be good Christian parents?

How can we as a Baptist denomination help students make the right Christian decisions? We have churches, the Bible, the Holy Spirit, and Christ's command:

> "*All power is given unto me in heaven and in earth. Go you therefore, and teach all nations, (and students) baptizing them in the name of the Father, and of the Son, and of the Holy Ghost. Teaching them to observe all things whatsoever I have commanded you: and, lo, I am with you always, even unto the end of the world.*" Matthew 28:18-20

The secret of success in student ministry is prayer and a daily intimate conversation with Jesus. Through prayer Jesus will give you what you need to carry out His will in leading students to know Christ and for them to make Him known.

> "*Whoever serves, let him do so as by the strength which God supplies; so that in all things God may be glorified through Jesus Christ. To Him be glory and dominion forever and ever.*" 1 Peter 5:11

HOW TO GET ORGANIZED AND STARTED

1. Make a prospect list of all Baptist students on your campus. Contact all the Baptist churches in your Baptist Association for names and addresses of students from their churches who are going to your college.
2. Ask the college enrollment department for a list of names and addresses of all Baptist students, or a list of all students.
3. Put an article in the Baptist state paper asking churches to send you the names and address of students who are attending your college.
4. Write a form letter addressed to each student introducing yourself to them and telling them that you would like for them to be a part of the BSU activities.
5. Set up an e-mail address and a web-site telling them about the program.
6. Set up an organization, with the campus minister as advisor. Appoint a nominating committee of three seniors and a Baptist faculty member

to conduct a student election with at least one person for each position, with a blank place for a write-in by each position.

President: in charge of Baptist Student Council activities
Vice president: in charge of enlistment and evangelism
Social Chair: in charge of recreation and food
Devotional Chair: in charge of prayer mates, noonday vespers, dorm Bible studies, and prayer groups
Music Chair: in charge of enlisting and leading students in music
Publicity Chair: editor, secretary, in charge of e-mail and web-site
Baptist Faculty Advisor
Local Pastor Advisor

These positions comprise the **Executive Council.** The **Greater Council** would be made up of five additional students under each of the student Executive Council members with the approval of the campus minister. The Executive Council is to meet for one hour every week and the Greater Council would meet once a month to plan Jesus Christ's program for the month.

The campus minister would have a planned 15 minute conference time each week with each individual Executive Council chairman to discuss the events for the next week. Each student would serve for one year and there would be new elections each year in April before the Spring State BSU Retreat.

In the fall, the Executive Council members will select new freshmen to serve on their committees with the approval of the campus minister. These freshmen will make up the **Freshman Council**, and serve to enlist other freshmen in the BSU activities. Other executive positions can be added as the need arises.

The Faculty Advisor will help the Executive Student Council members to understand the rules and operations of the faculty and the administration and how they can minister to them. If there is a non-Christian faculty member who tries to tear down a student's Christian beliefs, the Faculty Advisor would be the one the student could go to and get counseling on how one could build that course of study on top of his Christian convictions without losing faith.

The Pastor advisor would represent all the pastors in that community. He should be a member of the Associational Student Committee that provides money from the churches for the expenses of programs for the campus ministry. Some campus ministries are asking their alumni to give over and above their tithe to their church to help support the expenses of campus programs.

FACULTY AND ADMINISTRATION

It is very important for you to have a good relationship with the faculty and administration staff. Make a list of the entire Baptist faculty and learn their names and what churches they attend. Use them in your programs and volunteer your services when the opportunity arrives. I know of one BSU Director who was asked to be the chaplain of the university football team.

Have a monthly or quarterly faculty fellowship meeting with a different member giving his testimony or sharing a book with the group. Follow up with questions or comments. Check with the administration to see if they would like for you to volunteer to teach a credit course on the Gospel of John two days a week. Nominate the most active church member who is a faculty member for election by the students to serve as the Faculty Advisor on the Executive Council. He or she could organize and promote a monthly faculty administration seminar to meet in the Baptist Student Center or a local church on the first Thursday of each month at 3:30 p.m. for refreshments and 4:00 p.m. for a message on "The Case for Christ" and 4:30-5:00 for discussion and answer time. Other topics could be one of C S Lewis' books, and a Moody Bible Film on creation. Send out personal invitations to all faculty and administration staff. Ask a church member who is on the staff at the campus hospital to call your office when there is a faculty or student in the hospital that needs a visit.

THE HOLY SPIRIT, THE BIBLE, AND THE CHURCH

Three elements to success in student work are the Holy Spirit, the Bible, and the Church. If we are weak on any one of these three elements, we will not have a balanced program and we will not be doing all that God empowers and commands us to be and do.

The Holy Spirit is the head of the church and the interpreter of the Word of God. Jesus said, "*He that believeth on me, the works that I do shall he do also, and greater works than these shall he do; because I go to my Father" John 14:12*. Jesus is not limited to one body. He is in the heart of every believer. The Holy Spirit convicts of sin, and then leads one to salvation and a righteous relationship with Christ. The Holy Spirit's purpose is to glorify Christ and help us to do His work on the college and university campuses. "*For God has not given to us the spirit of fear; but of power, and of love, and of a sound mind" II Timothy I: 7.*

The Bible is the Word of God. "*All scripture is given by inspiration of God, and is profitable for doctrine, for reproof, for correction, for instruction in righteousness:*

That the man of God may be perfect, thoroughly furnished unto all good works" II Timothy 3:16. This is one of the goals of Campus Ministry. God speaks to us through His Word.

> "The Bible reveals the mind of God, the state of man, the way of salvation, the doom of sinners, and the happiness of believers. Its doctrines are holy, its precepts binding, its histories are true, and its decisions are immutable. Read it to be wise, believe it to be safe, and practice it to be holy. It contains light to direct you, food to support you, and comfort to cheer you. It is the traveler's map, the pilgrim's staff, the pilot's compass, the soldier's sword, and the Christian's charter.
>
> In the Bible, heaven is opened and the gates of hell disclosed. Christ is its grand subject; our good is its design, the glory of God its end. It should fill your memory, rule your heart, and guide the feet. Read it, slowly, frequently, and prayerfully. It is given in life, will be opened in the judgment, and will be remembered forever. It involves the highest responsibility, will reward the greatest labor, and will condemn all those who trifle with its sacred contents. Owned, it is riches; studied, it is wisdom; trusted, it is salvation; loved, it is character; and

obeyed, it is power." Author unknown (Billy Graham book marker)

Jesus built His Church to be composed of all who made the same confession of faith that Peter made: "*Thou art the Christ the Son of the living God*" *Matt.16:16*. The Church was built to carry on the mission that Jesus came to earth to do. Jesus said, "*For the Son of man is come to seek and to save that which was lost*" (Luke 19:10). The Church is God's foundation to carry on His work of redeeming the people of this world and the foundation is built on the Word of God, the Bible. A Southern Baptist church is autonomous and democratic in its origination with each member having one vote. The churches in a community work together to carry out Christ's great commission. Jesus said,

> *"All power is given unto me in heaven and in earth. Go you therefore, and teach all nations baptizing them in the name of the Father, and of the Son, and of the Holy Ghost. Teaching them to observe all things whatsoever I have commanded you: and, lo I am with you always, even unto the end of the world." Matthew 28: 18-20.*

Every Baptist church should be ministering to and with college students. **The Baptist campus ministry**

is the church reaching out to the campus during the week. The campus ministry should encourage students to be active in a local church on Wednesday and all day Sunday. Students are the future leaders of our churches, cities, businesses, and government.

BAPTIST CHURCHES WORK TOGETHER TO DO CHRIST'S WORK

"Jesus came to seek and to save that which was lost" Luke 19:10.

The church is God's foundation to win people to Christ. Every Baptist church needs to have in their Baptist Association an **Associational College Committee** to work with campus ministries on campuses where their students go to college or university. The **Baptist Association of Churches** needs to provide money for an active Christian program for reaching, winning, and disciplining students for the Lord. Every **Baptist State Convention** should have a **State Student Department** to promote a campus ministry on every college and university in the state. The State Convention needs to have a state Director of Campus Ministry to give leadership to each campus minister on each campus. The Baptist State Convention's goal should be to employ a campus minister for each campus with the approval of the Baptist Association Student Committee near that campus or university.

The Baptist Student Union Advancement Fund Program uses its funds to assist Baptist student ministries in areas where there is a special need. In 2010, the Foundation gave money to collegiate ministries in Hawaii, Indiana, New York, Utah/Idaho, Iowa, Minnesota/Wisconsin, New England, the Northwest, Ohio, Pennsylvania/South Jersey, Illinois, and California. If you would like to support the fund, send a contribution to the BSU ADVANCEMENT FUND on the internet. If you are working with a student ministry in an emerging region, contact your State Director of Baptist Collegiate Ministries about submitting a request for assistance next year. As the fund grows, more grants will be available. Most importantly, pray for the expansion of a Christian witness on campuses across North America.

JUNIOR COLLEGE MINISTRY

Junior college ministry is very important because a junior college campus minister can reach as great, if not a greater, percentage of his or her campus than a campus director on a four-year campus. There is often a closer relationship with students and not nearly as many distractions. The first two years of students' college lives are a very important time for them to establish a good Christian foundation. Students in junior colleges are often closer to their local churches on the weekends. Baptist Associational Pastors can be more involved and know the students who are from their churches. Program expenses are often less, and parents who live nearby can open their homes for social activities.

> *"Train up a (student) in the way he should go and when he is old, he will not depart from it" Proverbs 22:6.*

God's word tells us to:

"Let the word of Christ dwell in you (our students) richly in all wisdom: teaching and admonishing one another in\ psalms and hymns and spiritual songs, singing with grace in your hearts to the Lord. And whatsoever you do in word or deed, do all in the name of the Lord Jesus, giving thanks to God and the Father by him." Colossians 3: 16-1.

The Baptist Student Union is God's gift to college students. Through this organization, or movement, thousands of students have found the following: God as revealed in Christ; the real meaning of life; friendships that last a lifetime; God's will for their life in a chosen vocation; a Christian friendship that grew into a marriage and a Christian home; and a place of service and leadership that helped them to become outstanding Christian leaders in politics, science, medicine, business, community affairs and in the church.

The BSU is a student-led organization with a weekday campus program of religious education and a weekend program related to a Baptist church. Through this student movement, students can find friends, Christian recreation, prayer partners, discussion groups, music programs, and places of service that will help them to grow and develop into mature Christian leaders.

CHRISTIAN LEADERSHIP METHODS AND TECHNIQUES

"Wisdom is the principal thing, therefore get wisdom: and with all thy getting get understanding" Proverbs 4:7.

A major goal of campus ministry is to develop Christian leaders to know the Lord and make Him known to others. The student organization is designed to promote the importance of self-development and leadership. The idea is set forth by emphasizing good leadership through the application of learned techniques and skills. Leadership can best be measured in terms of results—in terms of what it accomplishes. Leadership is the directing of activities of other persons and the undertaking of responsibilities for achieving specified results through these efforts, while good Christian personality traits indicate more or less who a person is.

There are three fundamental skills that indicate what a person can do. Successful leadership appears to depend upon these three basic skills:

1. Technical skill
2. Human skill
3. Conceptual skill

Technical skill, simply stated, means one has the ability to perform some technical activities. One is proficient in a specific kind of activity. One understands the methods, processes, procedures, or techniques of the activity. The most effective way to gain technical skill seems to be for a student to study the principles, structures, and processes while working with a skilled person in a teacher-pupil relationship. (In a student-led organization this could be a senior leading a freshman, sophomore or junior.) Listed below are some processes, procedures and techniques in campus ministry (BSU) work in which a person can become proficient:

—Presiding and moderating a council meeting
—Conducting and planning a committee meeting
—Knowing the components of a good BSU meeting
—Enlisting and involving students
—Coordinating with the BSU and church activities
—Planning and projecting a mission project
—Building attendance at the meetings.

Human skills are skills of understanding and motivating individuals and groups. A student must develop his or her Christian point of view toward human activity so that the student will recognize the feelings and sentiments that he or she brings to a situation. Students must also develop the ability to successfully communicate their ideas and attitudes to others. This skill must be naturally developed and unconsciously demonstrated in every action. Human skill is accepting viewpoints, perceptions and beliefs that are different from one's own, so one is skillful in understanding what others really mean by their words and behavior.

Conceptual skill is coordinating and integrating all the activities and interests of the organization toward a common objective. It involves seeing the whole picture, recognizing how the various functions of the organization depend on one another, and understanding how changes in any one part affect all the others. It extends to visualizing the relationship of the individual organization to the university, church, community, and the political, social, and economic forces of the nation and world. Recognizing these relationships and perceiving the significant elements in any situation, the leader should be able to act in a way that advances the overall good of the total organization.

DISCIPLESHIP TRAINING

"Teaching them to observe all things whatsoever I have commanded you; and lo I am with you always, even unto the end of the world." Matthew 28:20

One needs to have a regular comprehensive teacher training program for students who want to grow in God's grace and knowledge. A suggested time could be Tuesday or Thursday from 4:00 to 5:00 p.m. every week. Find a different leader in each subject matter. Select from your pastors, staff members, Baptist faculty members, deacons, Christian business owners, or a Christian married couple to lead the study and discussion.

Possible topics include:

1. Experiencing God: A 12 week film and study book by Dr. Henry Blackaby
2. Biblical Doctrines
3. Courtship, Marriage and Family
4. Stewardship and Finances
5. Spiritual Gifts

6. How to Share the Gospel
   a. The Roman Road Plan of Salvation
   b. Friendship Witnessing
   c. Four Spiritual Laws

7. How the Holy Spirit Convicts of Sin and Reveals Jesus

One example of a possible study lesson is included below.

How to Respond to Faith Challenges

Purpose:

To provide simple statements that a Christian can use in response to challenges to the faith posed by non-Christians.

Motivation:

Many times a Christian is challenged with probing questions by skeptics. This is most apparent for college students as they leave home for college. Inability to respond appropriately can lead to, at a minimum, a weakening of a student's faith and testimony. At worst, it can lead to a total falling away from the faith. Weak and ineffectual responses reinforce skeptics in their unbelief.

<u>Style of Presentation</u>:

The responses listed below are in the form of simple bullet point statements. Theological terminology is minimized. Along with the responses are questions that the Christian should ask the skeptic that are designed to challenge and cause them to question their beliefs.

<u>Hints for the Christian</u>:

Responses should be offered boldly yet in a gentle non-confrontational manner. Many times the motivation underlying skeptics' challenges are based more on individuals wanting to maintain their present lifestyle, which is inconsistent with Christianity. Emphasize what one is gaining in Christ rather than what they are giving up. It is not enough to convince a person for the need of God in their life because the individual may go off and define his own convenient God. What is important is to emphasize Jesus and salvation through Him! Whenever and wherever possible, mention Jesus Christ more than terms like Lord and God, as these latter terms may have different meanings to different people.

Challenge: Why does God allow evil to exist?

Response:

- Evil exists already, God does not want it and He is grieved by it.

- God brings good to an evil world. God allows evil in the first place because He endows men and women with the ability to make free choices (free will).
- The source of the worst evil has been atheism.
- God's will is designed for people's benefit: to give one purpose, strength, and direction, and eventually an eternal home with God.
- Given free will, a person chooses after his or her own selfish desires. This is disobedience and rebellion against God's will. This is called sin.
- Imagine God getting rid of all evil. None of us could commit any evil . . . We would have no liberty to decide our wants and want nots . . . Our desires and choices would be God's and not our own . . . We would no longer be created beings in the image of God, having the power of choice . . . We would be like puppets, dolls, or robots incapable of loving God back.
- God could not have a personal relationship with us based on our trust in Him.
- Evil grieves God so much that He personally came down in the form of a man, Jesus, to personally provide a model of "good." God's prescription for good is revealed through Jesus and the Bible. Through Jesus we can be delivered from the consequences of our disobedience and sin.

Questions for the skeptic to answer:

- What about all the good that God blesses us with?
- What would change in your life if no evil existed?
- Would you want to live the life of a robot?

Challenge: Religion has been the greatest cause of wars and misery to mankind.

Response:

- Wrong, the greatest cause of wars and human misery has been atheism. Just in the 19th century alone there have been more war deaths and human misery caused by atheistic powers than all the so-called religious-based wars in all of human history (Example = Stalin).
- Even many of the so-called wars of religion were based on selfishness of power and riches masquerading as religion.
- Religion (especially Christianity) has been one of the greatest sources of benefit to humans. Example: The establishment of hospitals and institutions of higher learning.
- Few, if any of the atheistic powers in history bothered with alleviating the plight of the common man, especially if no profit was involved.

Questions for the skeptic to answer:

- Can you pinpoint something you have done to help alleviate human misery?
- Would you prefer a Godless world where there are no moral absolutes, no restraints, and any behavior is permissible because there is no right or wrong??

Challenge: Why does God allow little children to have terminal illnesses?

Response:

- It is human's selfish desire that is the basis for essentially all human misery. Selfish desires apply not only at the seats of power but also at the individual level.
- Example: Many young scientists, who are endowed by God with great intelligence and talent, decide to apply their talents to higher paying, less demanding, less time-consuming careers, rather than at the frontier of medical research. Illnesses like cancer could have been cured by now if as many resources were applied to it as we apply, for instance to dog food, or cosmetics, not to mention wars. Many illnesses are caused by people's poor choices in life, ignorance, and/or negligent behavior.
- Examples: Subjecting babies to second-hand smoke; drinking or taking drugs during

pregnancy; living on land previously used secretly as a toxic waste dump; exposure to cancer-causing agents at a job by negligent employers.

- The loss of a loved one is a tragedy for us, but in Christianity it is a gain for the lost one.
- Our view of the current life is incomplete. Death is not the end. God has a plan for us that extends into eternity.

Questions for the skeptics to answer:

- If you had a terminal illness and were offered a sure cure, would you accept it?
- Separation from God is a terminal illness, Jesus is the sure cure.
- Are you absolutely sure that your beloved child will go to a place of rest and bliss (in Heaven) upon their death?

Challenge: The church is full of hypocrites.

Response:

- We are all hypocrites to one extent or another. Some hypocrisy is more obvious and/ outrageous than others. We have a vision (or model) of what is acceptable or advantageous behavior and we act it out for whatever advantage, selfish or unselfish, as it may be. Hypocrisy in others usually does not rule our lives.

- Examples: We don't quit our jobs because our boss or fellow workers are hypocrites . . . We go to, and enjoy ballgames, theaters, etc. even though the persons next to us may be hypocrites, or are there for some other ulterior motive . . .
- The blessings found in the Lord greatly outweigh any disappointment possibly seen in others.
- Christians go to church to worship God, to have fellowship with others, and to grow spiritually. We avoid being judgmental of those around us.
- The Christian experience is looking up to God rather than judging others. The basis for evaluating Christ is Christ . . . not Christians.
- The great majority of the Christians are alike. They recognize their weaknesses and look to the Lord to mold our lives closer and closer to Jesus.
- Many atheist and agnostics claim they are just being honest and do not want to be hypocritical. Yet, to some extent or other, we are all hypocrites.
- Our Lord Jesus said that He came to minister to the unrighteous.
- To state that we are not unrighteous is, in fact, hypocrisy.
- There is a lot more hypocrisy outside the church than there is inside the church.

- Even if there are hypocrites in church, it is better to spend time with a few of them now, rather than spend eternity with all the rest of them.

Questions for the skeptic to answer:

- Please tell me about your experience with hypocrites in church? I have never really had a problem with hypocrisy or hypocrites even in many years of being active in church. Note: Many individuals present the hypocrisy challenge even though it is hearsay and they don't have first-hand experience.
- Isn't a hospital the place to go if you are sick? Or do you refuse to go to a hospital when ill because there are so many sick people there?
- Isn't the church the place to go in order to grow spiritually, emotionally and psychologically—a place to be if you recognize your limitations?
- Should you be judgmental of those that need the Lord and express it by exercising Christian beliefs?
- Are you absolutely sure of your own ability to improve yourself on your own?
- Do you deny the many great people that have made significant contributions due to their Christian faith (as Dr. Billy Graham and C. S. Lewis and thousands of other missionaries and Christian leaders).

SPIRITUAL MATURITY AND SPIRITUAL WISDOM

Where are you in your Christian life and understanding of God's word and will for your life? First, it is essential that we are born again. Apart from spiritual birth there can be no spiritual maturity.

> *"Being born again, not of corruptible seed, but of incorruptible, by the Word of God, which liveth and abideth forever." 1 Peter 1:23*

Just as a human baby has two parents, so a spiritual baby has two parents—the **Word of God and the Spirit of God.** How, then is a person "born again"? The Spirit of God takes the Word of God and generates new life within the heart of the sinner who believes on Jesus Christ. It is a miracle. The Spirit uses the Word to convict the sinner, and then to reveal the Savior. We are saved by faith (Eph. 2:8-9) and faith comes by hearing the Word of God (Romans 10:17).

Second, to become mature we must examine our life in the light of God's Word. James 1:22 tells us to "*be you doers of the word, and not hearers only, deceiving your own selves.*" As we study the Word of God, we are looking into the divine mirror and seeing ourselves as we really are. But James warns us that we must be honest about what we see and not merely glance at the image and walk away.

Have you heard about the primitive man who looked into a mirror for the first time? He was so shocked at what he saw that he broke the mirror! Many people make the same mistake—after hearing God's word they criticize the preacher or the Bible, when they ought to be judging themselves and growing in maturity.

The third essential is to obey what God teaches us no matter what the cost. We must be "doers of the word and not hearers only." It is easy to attend a Bible study, share the lesson and discuss it, but it is much more difficult to go out into life in the work-a-day world and practice what we have learned. The blessing does not come in studying the Word, but in doing the Word. Unless we are willing to obey, the Lord is not obligated to teach us, or help us develop into maturity.

James 1:5 says "*If any of you lack **wisdom**, let him ask of God, that giveth to all men liberally, and upbraideth not, and it will be given to him.*" By wisdom, James is talking not only about knowledge, but about the ability to make wise decisions in difficult circumstances. Whenever we need wisdom, we can pray to God and He will generously supply what we need. Christians don't have to grope around in the dark, hoping for the right answers. We can ask for God's wisdom to guide our choices. **Wisdom means practical discernment**. It begins with respect for God, leads to right living, and results in increased ability to tell right from wrong. God is willing to give us this wisdom, but we will be unable to receive it if our goals are self-centered instead of God-centered. To learn God's will, we need to read His Word and ask Him to show us how to obey it.

TRUE LOVE WAITS

"True love waits" means that my body is the temple of the Holy Spirit and I promise God and myself that I will keep my body pure and clean until I get married because that is the will and purpose of God for me. "*Thy word have I hid in my heart that I will not sin against Thee*" Psalm 119: 11. God's purpose for a Christian marriage is for a man and woman to leave father and mother and be united to each other and they will become one flesh until death.

If one is not willing to control their emotions and fleshly desires until marriage, then it is not true love. True love is mature, wholesome and pure. It is worth waiting for marriage when both husband and wife have true love for the rest of their lives together. Every Christian has the Holy Spirit in his or her heart and the power of God to resist every temptation. God promises in I Cor. 10:13 that "*No temptation has seized you except what is common to man. And God is faithful, and He will not let you be tempted beyond what you can bear. But when you are tempted, He will also provide a way out so that you can stand under it*"

(NIV). Marriage is for a lifetime on earth, so be sure and make the right choice with God's help.

Every campus ministry program should have an emphasis on this commitment and cards for students to make their pledge to dedicate their life to the purpose and goal of "True Love Waits."

MARRIED STUDENTS' CHRISTIAN SEMINARS

Married students have many needs that we can provide for with God's help. They have a need for Christian fellowship with other married Baptist students. They have a need for good Christian counseling about the six issues listed below. Discussion questions for each topic are also listed.

1. Marriage Relationships and Building on Commitments

a. Should our marriage be built on love or commitments?
b. Should our relationships be 50-50 or 100-100%?
c. What is the best way to work out the leadership role in different activities in the family?
d. Does God give each person different spiritual gifts?

e. Who is responsible for the training, discipline, and the good-nature of the children?
f. What should we watch and not watch on TV, internet, and movies? What are the dangers?
g. How can we develop a greater respect and devotion for each other?
h. What is the most effective way to witness to someone in the family who is not a Christian?
i. What are some good ways of having time for Bible reading, quiet time with Jesus, or family worship time?
j. How important should the Church be in your spiritual growth and worship of Jesus?

2. Budgeting and Financing

a. What is the best way to keep money from dividing the family?
b. What is the best way to use credit cards to keep from going in debt?
c. What is the best way to set up a budget for the family? For each individual?
d. What are the best arrangements when both mates have incomes?
e. When should you have insurance? Car, home or renters, life, or health?

f. How important is the selection of a job? Travel, dangers, time out of town, honesty, relationships, and health?
g. Should you tithe to your church? Do you want God to bless you in your stewardship of life?
h. Should you budget for savings, (sick days, out of work, vacation, baby, home, etc.)?
i. How much do you believe in God's promises of Matthew 6:33 and Romans 8:28?

3. Planning for Children and Childcare

a. What do the local Baptist churches offer in childcare and baby care?
b. What things should be considered about planning for children while going to college or working full-time?
c. What are the joys of having a baby when the time is right?
d. What are the basic costs to plan for as you plan for each child?
e. What are the dangers of having an abortion?
f. How do you adopt a child?
g. What are the best books and information on raising children?

h. What are the best times to teach a child to pray and have a personal relationship with Jesus?
i. How important is it to read to your child?
j. What is the best way to teach your children to use the computer in the right way?

4. Food and Exercise and Taking Care of Your Body, The Temple of the Holy Spirit

"Know you not that your body is the temple of the Holy Spirit which is in you, which you have of God, and you are not your own? For you are bought with a price: therefore glorify God in your body, and in your spirit, which are God's" 1 Corinthians 6: 19-20.

a. What exercises are the best for one to keep his or her body in good health?
b. What foods are best to keep one's body in good health?
c. How can we glorify God in our bodies and control our sex desires?
d. What place does prayer have in helping one to get well, or stay healthy?
e. When a couple gets married how do they become one in spirit and relationship? Ephesians 4:2-7

f. How important are organic foods considering the difference in price?
g. What are the dangers of smoking? Even second-hand smoke?
h. What is the best way to help a person who is begging for money for food?

5. Vocation and the Use of Time

a. Does God have a plan and purpose for one's life?
b. How can one find out about his or her spiritual gifts?
c. How can one develop a good balance between work, study, family, church, recreation and sleep?
d. How do you select the job that you will spend your life doing? Is the most important aspect purpose, happiness, honesty, health, relationships, income, time, or contribution to the Kingdom of God and humanity?
e. Should one invest his or her life in money and things or in people, who will be eternal?
f. What are the advantages and disadvantages of both husband and wife working outside the home?
g. How much time should be set aside for devotional quiet time of Bible reading, relationship time with your spouse, three

meals a day, sleep, church, house work, vocation, exercise, and children when they come?

h. Are you using your vocation skills and talents for the glory of God and His kingdom, such as singing in the church choir, teaching a Sunday School class, serving on a church committee, witnessing on visitation, tithing, and mission trips?

6. Spiritual Growth

a. How important is God in your life?
b. How can the church help you in your spiritual growth?
c. Do you have a personal relationship with Jesus as your Lord and Savior?
d. What is your favorite scripture verse? Does this verse express your philosophy of life?
e. Do you believe that Jesus answers prayers?
f. What is the best way for one to share his or her faith in Jesus Christ with someone else?
g. How does the Holy Spirit work in a Christian's life?
h. What are the advantages of being a member of a local church where you worship?
i. Why should a believer be baptized into the fellowship of a church?

j. Do you believe the Bible is the inspired Word of God?
k. Do you know for sure that when you die you will go to heaven?

MARRIED STUDENTS WITH CHILDREN ARE GOD'S BABYSITTERS

One of the loveliest incidents in the Gospel is when the mothers brought the children to Jesus that He might touch them. No wonder they wished Jesus to lay his hand on their children. They had seen what those hands could do; they had seen Him touch disease and pain away; had seen those hands bring sight to the blind eyes, and peace to the mind; and they wanted hands like that to touch their children. There is a loveliness about Jesus Christ that anyone can see as you read about Him and experience him in your life. It is easy to think of these mothers of Palestine feeling that the touch of a man like that on their children's heads would bring a blessing, even if they did not understand why.

The disciples of Jesus wanted to protect Jesus. The disciples saw how tired Jesus was; they saw what healing cost him. He was talking to them so often about the cross, and they must have seen on his face the tension of his heart and soul. They could not conceive that he could want the children about him at such a time as that. But in Mark 10:14 – 16, Jesus said,

> *"Suffer the little children to come unto me, and forbid them not: for of such is the Kingdom of God. Verily I say unto you, whosoever shall not receive the Kingdom of God as a little child, he shall not enter therein. And he took them up in his arms, put his hands upon them, and blessed them."*

This story tells us a great deal about Jesus. It tells us that he was the kind of person who cared for children and for whom children cared. There must have been a kindly sunshine on him. He must have smiled easily and laughed joyously. To Jesus no one was unimportant. He was never too tired, never too busy to give all of himself to anyone who needed him. Jesus said of the children that they were nearer to God than anyone else there. The child's simplicity is closer to God than anything else. It is life's tragedy that as we grow older, we so often grow further from God rather than nearer to Him.

Jesus tells his babysitters of the child-like qualities of one in the Kingdom of God. The child has not lost the sense of wonder as he or she discovers God's beautiful world. The child lives in a world with a brightness on it and in which God is always near. The child's whole life is founded on trust. When we are young, we never doubt where the next meal is to come from or where our clothes will be found. We go to school certain that home will be there when we return, and all things ready for our comfort. The child's trust in his or her parents is absolute, as ours should be in our Father—God.

In every child there are infinite possibilities for good or bad. It is the supreme responsibility of the parents to see that the child's dynamic possibilities for good are realized. To stifle them, to leave them untapped, to twist them into evil powers, is sin. Once a man consulted a psychiatrist about the best thing he could do for his children. He had made a list, including such things as food, clothes, house, assuring an opportunity for education; making available religious training; instilling in the children proper social attitudes; and setting a good moral example. The psychiatrist said, "All these are extremely important, but you have not named the most important thing you can do for your children." The man wondered aloud what was more important than the things he had named. The psychiatrist said, "The best thing you can do for your children is to **love their mother**." I think that is a wise statement, because children are alive to the kind of affection there is between father and mother. Nothing gives them a deeper sense of security than to know their parents love each other. Nothing shakes them quite as much as to realize love is lacking between the two adults they depend on the most.

THE IMPORTANCE OF JESUS IN YOUR LIFE

Without Jesus you can do nothing of importance that is lasting.

> "*With Jesus you can do all things that Christ would have you do*" Matthew 19:26.
>
> "*In the beginning was the Word (Jesus), and the Word (Jesus) was God*" John 1:1.
>
> "*All things were made by Jesus; and without Him was not anything made that was made*" John 1: 3.

Genesis 1:26 tell us that Jesus created us in His own image so we could have fellowship with Him. Jesus came to earth in the form of man and lived a perfect life. Galatians 4:4 tells us that He then paid the penalty for the sins of all those who will accept Him as Lord of their life by faith.

> "*If anyone be in Christ Jesus he is a new person, old things have passed away. Behold all things have become new*" II Cor. 5:17.

> Jesus said, "*I am the way, the truth, and the life and no one comes to the Father except through me*" John 14:6.

> "*There is no other name given among men whereby we must be saved except through Jesus*" Acts 4: 12.

Jesus wants to be your best friend, your savior, your Lord and master, your advocate, making intercessions for you, "*and the justifier of the one who has faith in Jesus*" (Romans 3: 26). He also wants to be your great physician and healer, comforter, peace and joy (Luke 4:18). Jesus will be your resurrection, redeemer, judge, rewarder, and eternal God.

> "*Therefore seeing we also are compassed about with so great a cloud of witnesses, let us lay aside every weight, and the sin which doth so easily beset us, and let us run with patience the race that is set before us, looking unto Jesus the author and finisher of our faith, who for the joy that was set before him endured the cross, despising the shame, and is set down at the right hand of the throne of God*" Hebrews 12: 1-2.

THE STORY IS TOLD OF GOD'S GRACE

A mother wishing to encourage her young son's progress on the piano took the small boy to a Paderewski concert. After they were seated the mother spotted a friend in the audience and walked down the aisle to greet her. Seizing the opportunity to explore the wonders of the concert hall, the little boy rose and eventually explored his way through a door marked "No Admittance". When the house lights dimmed and the concert was about to begin, the mother returned to her seat and discovered that her son was missing.

Suddenly, the curtains parted and spotlights focused on the impressive Steinway on stage. In horror, the mother saw her little boy sitting at the keyboard, innocently picking out "Twinkle, Twinkle Little Star." At that moment, the great piano master made his entrance, quickly moved to the piano, and whispered in the boy's ear, "Don't quit, keep playing." Then leaning over, Paderewski reached down with his left hand and began filling in a bass part. Soon his right arm reached around to the other side of the child and he added a running obligato. Together, the old master and the young novice transformed a frightening situation into a wonderfully creative experience. The audience was mesmerized.

That's the way it is with God. What we can accomplish on our own is hardly noteworthy. We try our best, but the results aren't exactly graceful flowing music. But with the hand of the Master, our life's work truly can be beautiful. The next time you set out to accomplish great feats, listen carefully. You can hear the voice of the Master, whispering in your ear, "Don't quit, keep playing." Feel His arms around you. Know that His strong hands are playing the concerto of your life.

Remember, God doesn't call the equipped, He equips the called. Your worst days are never so bad that you are beyond the reach of God's Grace. And your best days are never so good that you are beyond the need of God's Grace.

THE GREATNESS OF GOD

I want you to see and experience the greatness of God and His love for each of us. Let us look at two chapters in the Bible, John 14 and Revelations 21 to see the greatness and the love of God and to see what God has in store for each of us. Jesus said in John 14:1 "*Let not your heart be troubled: believe in God, believe also in me.*" Most people do believe in a god or gods. Buddhist, Hindus, and Moslems believe in religious leaders and many claim these as their god, but they are all dead and God did not raise any of them from the dead, and none of them died to save any one from their sins.

The Bible tells us in Romans chapter 1 that people can see God in nature, but they worship what God created rather than worshipping the God of creation, their Creator. Who do you worship? Is it money, work, your children, or yourself?

People who believe in evolution rather than **creation** do not know how great God really is. When God created the world in the beginning He could have made rocks and formations a million years old or any age He wanted them to be, or He could have created the stars and planets with light rays just right for us to live on this planet Earth, and He did it all in six days. That is how great our God is. If we would realize how great our God is, who is revealed in the Bible, and in Jesus the Christ, we would realize that nothing is impossible with God. Many people of the world do not understand who the one and only true God is. We send missionaries around the world to tell everyone who the true God is so they can believe in the true living God, who can save us from our sins.

In the fullness of time God sent forth His Son so that whoever believes in Him should not perish in their sins, but would have eternal life, and fellowship with a holy and righteous God. This is why Jesus paid the penalty for our sins by His death on the cross and His resurrection, and made it possible for us to live forever with Him in heaven.

Jesus told His disciples in John 14:11, "*Believe Me that I am in the Father and the Father in Me, or else believe me for the very works' sake.*" Look at what Jesus did. Jesus healed the sick, the blind, the lame, and the dead. Jesus healed the sin-sick souls and transformed them to be children of God. Jesus died on the cross for our sins and then He rose from the dead to be the Savior for all who will believe in Him for eternal life and forgiveness of their sin. Jesus sent the Holy Spirit to live in the heart of every believer. Jesus is given all authority in Heaven and on Earth to evangelize the world. Jesus goes to prepare a place in heaven for each believer. Jesus is at the right hand of God the Father making intercession for all believers. Jesus has promised to come again to judge everyone and to give all whose name is written in the Book of Life a resurrected body for eternity.

I cannot understand why everyone is not a born-again Christian, even if there was not life after death, because the abundant life of fellowship with Christ and Christians is so great, even on the earth. But the best is yet to come. Look at how much God loves you. He wants to have a personal relationship with you for eternity. In John 14:2 Jesus says,

> "*In My Father's house are many mansions: if it were not so, I would have told you: for I go to prepare a place for you. And if I go and prepare a place for you, I will come again, and receive you to Myself; that where I am, there you may be also.*"

Heaven is more beautiful than you can ever imagine. Have you ever been to an event so wonderful you did not want it to ever end? Was it a musical, a revival, a banquet, a concert, a game, or fellowship with a group that you loved to be with? This is what Heaven is going to be like. If God can make a rainbow, a sunset, or a sunrise that is so beautiful on this earth, just think how beautiful the sky will be in heaven. All of this will be in Heaven, plus the beauty and joy of the faces of all the healthy Christians with the love of Christ glowing on their faces. (How old do you think we will be in our new resurrected bodies? My guess is around 33, the same age as Jesus at His ascension.)

The greatest thing about Heaven will be the personal relationship and fellowship with God the Father, Son, and Holy Spirit face to face. We will be able to sit at His feet and hear Him tell us all about the Kingdom of God. We can join the heavenly choir and sing praises to our Lord and Savior as we have never sung before (and never out of tune or pitch).

Are you sure you will go to Heaven when you die? You can know for sure. Choose this day who you will serve. Will it be Christ the Son of the living God who loves you and died on the cross for your sins? If you will ask Him to save you and come and live in your heart, He promises He will. If you do nothing, you will continue to serve Satan, because you are still in your sins, and the end is not heaven but the lake that burns with fire and brimstone, which is the second death forever.

God's Word promises that whosoever will call on the name of Jesus will be saved. Jesus is knocking at your heart's door. Will you invite Him into your life? Will you pray this prayer in your own words if you want Jesus to save you from your sins and give you eternal life?

"Lord Jesus, I need you to save me. Thank you for dying on the cross for my sins. I invite you into my heart and life and receive you as my Savior and Lord. Take control of the throne of my life, and make me the kind of person you want me to be." If you sincerely prayed that prayer from your heart you are now a child of God. Now you need to find a good Bible-preaching church and be baptized, and start growing as a Christian.

THE UNIVERSITY CAMPUS IS GOD'S MISSION FIELD

Ministry with International Students

Students have come to prepare for what they are to do for the rest of their lives. God has a plan and a purpose for everyone. A study from the Pew Forum on Religion and Public Life found that a large number of people now engage in multiple religious practices, mixing features of various faiths. Many blend Christianity with elements of Eastern and New Age beliefs, such as reincarnation, astrology, and even the occult religions. Because of this, many students are questioning whether Jesus Christ is really the only way to God.

If pollsters and students would ask Jesus that question, they would get a clear answer: "*I am the way, the truth, and the life. No one comes to the Father except through me*" (John 14:6, NIV). If they asked the apostle Peter or Luke, they would be told: "*Salvation is found in no one else, for there is no other name under heaven given to men by which we must be saved*" Acts 4:12. Going the wrong way down a one-way street is deadly. It doesn't matter how sincerely intentioned the driver is, or how educated, or how broad-minded—it can still get him or her killed. Don't try to paint over the one-way signs of scripture. Just make sure you're going the right way. Jesus is not one of many ways to approach God, He is the only way to God the Father.

While I was the Baptist Student Director at Mississippi State University I helped a Korean student get enrolled in the university. After many times of fellowship and witnessing, he asked Jesus to be his Lord and Master and save him from his sins. When he gave his testimony to the BSU group he said that he had always thought that Buddha was the God for Asia and Jesus was the God for the West, but now he knows that Jesus is the only God who can save one from his or her sins. When he graduated he went back to his country to be a witness for Christ.

God is sending the future leaders of the world to our colleges and universities for us to witness to them as Philip did to the Ethiopian, Acts 9.27. The International Mission Board says, "If you have worked with an International Student and the student is returning to their country, what better way to show them that you care than to have a missionary contact them when they get home?" All you have to do is tell the IMB how the student can be contacted and they will follow up the contact. Send information to Mike Lopez: E-Mail: mlopeq@imb.org.

Each semester we would try to have a banquet and invite all the international students on campus. We asked the university president, Dr. Rayburn, to be the main speaker because he was the Adult Sunday School teacher at the First Baptist Church, and he did a good job of presenting the gospel. This was also a good time to present each student with a new Bible.

Currently, 70% of Asian international university-educated believers hear the good news for the first time from their foreign teachers and leaders. International students are eager to learn English for the benefit of their economy and international relations. The Bible is a good resource for teaching the English language. God said, "I will bless you . . . and all peoples on earth will be blessed through you" Genesis 12:2-3, NIV.

MISSION OPPORTUNITIES

"Holy, Holy, Holy is the Lord of Host: the whole earth is full of his glory. Then said I, Woe is me! For I am undone; because I am a man of unclean lips, and I dwell in the midst of a people of unclean lips: for mine eyes have seen the King, the Lord of hosts . . . Also I heard the voice of the Lord, saying, Whom shall I send, and who will go for us? Then said I, Here am I; send me. And He said, Go, and tell this people, Hear ye indeed." Isaiah 6:3, 5, 8-9.

Christian students are the most effective witnesses to other students. Tell them what Jesus has done in your life, and what He is doing, and what He has promised in His word of what He will be doing in the future.

Baptist Student Mission Opportunities: Each year Mississippi State University BSU equips and sends students across the world for the cause of Christ. In 2009 they sent 20 students to countries in Asia. This is called their **Summer Missions** program. BSU'ers raise the funds to send their fellow BSU'ers who are chosen to go to our Baptist mission fields to work with our full-time missionaries.

Medical Mission Opportunities: Medical students, nurses, and Christian doctors volunteer to do free medical work with mission organizations worldwide.

Here are some suggestions for raising the funds:

1. Fund-raising through Youth Revival Team preaching on the weekends in rural churches
2. Supply preaching by students
3. Offerings from BSU-sponsored Vacation Bible Schools for children
4. Student pledges over and above their tithes to their churches
5. Silent Auction of gifts donated by merchants and students

North American Baptist Mission Ministries tells us there are 18 million collegiate students in North America and less than 15% profess to have a personal relationship with Jesus Christ. North American Baptist Mission Ministries want to be partners with all BSU'ers as they sponsor Beach Evangelism for students to witness to fellow students during school Spring Break each year. They also encourage students to sign up to do summer mission work during the summer months working with adult full-time Missionaries in North America.

The Baptist International Mission Ministries has a good program called the Journeyman Program for graduate students to be missionaries for two years with our overseas missionaries. Many of these come back to the States and go to the seminary to prepare to apply to be a full-time International Missionary.

MISSION TRIPS TO INDIA

The first time I heard about the group of people from our church going to India and how the Lord was blessing the people of India and blessing those who went, it made my heart want to go the next year. The next year, the doors would not open for me to go. Was I too old to go? Could the Lord still use me at age 87?

Then the next year I kept praying and typing out sermons and offering myself to the Lord, and God started opening the doors for me to go. My health and my wife's health were much better. The time to apply was near, so on faith I sent my $100 in to the church. Then I could not find my old passport to get a visa to go. I was in Alabama in September and the group was ready to go the first of November. We rushed back to Florida to get my papers in with no passport, visa or birth certificate.

On faith, I sent the letters out for my close friends and relatives to pray for me. The church office suggested that I go to Miami and apply for my passport and visa. The Lord opened the doors again and the papers went through just in time.

Working and witnessing with the team of 28 Americans and the Indian people gave me a boldness in witnessing that I had not had, as when April suggested during the invitation to invite the converts to pray the sinner's prayer, and they did.

This trip to India was the greatest spiritual experience of my life since my conversion experience 74 years before. The next two years, 2007 and 2008, I returned to do mission work in India with our church group and every year the Lord used us and blessed us more than we could ever dream possible. It is so wonderful to be a part of what God is doing in India. In 2008, God used our 11 teams to visit and preach in 102 villages with 35,000 hearing the gospel and 7,500 making new decisions for Christ. Twenty-three water wells were provided to needy villages, 4500 tooth brushes and salvation message bracelets distributed. We also gave 1650 bed sheets to senior citizens and pastors' families. God used us to do all this and much more in only ten days.

Another powerful experience was the Pastor's Seminar Conference for 315 village pastors and translators. We ended the week with a three day Crusade with around 40,000 in attendance and over 12,000 written decisions for Christ.

One of the greatest things our church, Boca Glades Baptist, has done is to buy two jeep station wagons and video projector equipment to show the Jesus video film in the villages. Our pastor, Truman Herring, wrote the book, "Challenge of John," to train the pastors in India to follow-up each showing with a six week study for the converts in their homes.

We are now sending money for Bible Schools to train pastors who will start a new church in their home or village. The first year we did this, the 25 Pastors who took the training started 35 new churches and baptized 2,000 new converts to Christ. So now we are expanding this program with many new Bible Schools for new pastors who will start a new church.

Pastor Truman Herring says that from a generous gift from a Christian brother we will lay the foundation for 4 schools with 100 pastors to be trained in our Bible Diploma Courses. The diploma is granted after a pastor completes the ten books and plants a new house church. We partner with TTI (The Timothy Initiative) and its founder, Dr. David Nelms, who will be going with us to introduce the church planting schools. Of all the things we have done in missions, I feel that this is our greatest investment. For an investment of $150 we provide a pastor with a solid Bible diploma and a new church start. This will mean that our church will have in just over one year provided 250 pastors in India, 120 pastors in Nagaland, and 100 pastors in Columbia with a Bible diploma with the expectations of at least 470 new church starts. When you add our totals to that of the entire TTI network, this will mean that over 7,000 new churches have been planted in Southeast Asia, Africa, and South America in just over 2 years. We need to praise the Lord Jesus Christ and the Holy Spirit for the wonderful work they are doing in the lives of these new pastors.

Roy Isbell preaching through an interpreter in India.

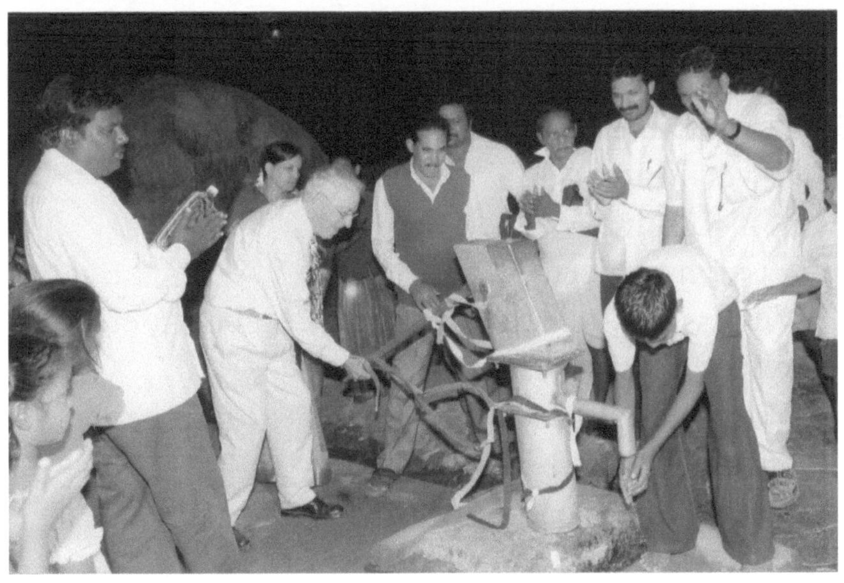

Roy Isbell Dedicating a Water Well in India

OTHER POSSIBLE BSU ACTIVITIES

1. Pre-semester retreat to plan the first month's activities and welcome freshman and new students
2. Devotional times:
   a. Daily, Monday—Friday 12:15-12:45 PM
   b. Noon meal on Wednesdays with devotion
   c. Thursday evening Vespers with praise and worship, 6:15-6:45 pm
3. Dorm Bible Study Groups, 10:00-10:30 pm
4. Prayer-Mates
5. BSU Choir
6. Mission projects
7. Witnessing—tracts, web-site, Facebook, etc.
8. Youth Revival Teams
9. International Hour and conversation partners
10. Summer Missions
11. Spring Break Mission Projects
12. Statewide BSU Convention
13. Nationwide BSU Week at Ridgecrest, NC or Glorietta, NM

14. Baptist World Youth Conference every five years
15. Weekly nursing home ministry
16. Community mission projects such as Big Brother/ Big Sister
17. Backyard Bible Study
18. Mission appointments in the U.S.A. or around the world
19. Supply Preaching
20. Monthly BSU Newsletter sent to all Baptist students
21. BSU Radio Program
22. Start a chapter of the Baptist Student Union on your campus if you do not have one

CHRIST'S CHURCH BUILDING A BETTER WORLD

I believe that God's word and church history tells us that God is working through His church and Christian organizations of the church to create a new society of Christian people to build a better world. Have you ever stopped to think about what God is seeking to accomplish in your life and in your church? God created man and woman in His own image so that He might have fellowship with them. From that time on, God has been revealing His love for man and woman. Even after Adam and Eve were disobedient to God, God has continued to reveal his love and plan of redemption: First, through the family of Adam and Eve, then through the tribe of Abraham, then through the nation of Israel, and finally through His church.

Because God is working uniquely through His church and we are members of His church, we need to think about three important questions:

1. Who are we?
2. What do we stand for?
3. Where are we going?

We need to think of these questions both as a member of the Church and as individual college Christians. First, let us look at who we are as a Church.

The Church is God's Creation. Jesus said He will build My Church on those who believe that Jesus is the Christ, the Son of the living God and the power of hell will not be able to stand against it. The church is the true Israel. The church was a continuation of ancient Israel, the inheritor of the promise to be God's children—God's chosen instrument to make known His will and His mercy.

By identifying the church as the true Israel, we mean that the church is not an institution, but the people of God; not an organization, but the body of Christ. As First Peter puts it: "*You are a chosen generation, a royal priesthood, a holy nation, a peculiar people*" 1 Peter 2: 9.

While the church is the true Israel, it is also a New Israel. God sought to fulfill His old covenant with Abraham through a new covenant in Christ with the people He had chosen and called forth. No longer was one incorporated into the body of His people by a natural birth, but rather by a New Birth. This is a second birth, a spiritual birth through faith in Christ.

It is a birth that re-orients, re-orders and re-makes one's life.

It was a new society, called the church, in the midst of the old society. It was a new society in which men and women were released from the yoke of bondage of sin by the grace of God in Jesus Christ, living under His rule and letting His teachings order their lives. A society or church that was both a sign and a foretaste of God's own kingdom in which His will would be done. The church then is the society, the fellowship, the community of all of those who are knit together in love through faith in Christ Jesus.

We have been talking about the universal church. Now look at the churches as an institution or as individual churches. What is the distinction between the two churches? The Universal or spiritual church is an end, a means, a pure fellowship, a communion of the saints, while the individual churches are institutions, organizations, ecclesiastical structures. The universal church had its beginning with creation, while the individual churches were brought into existence because the blessings of Christian fellowship were not to be once received and then passively enjoyed. These churches are missionary societies, seeking to transmit by word and by deed God's reconciling love to all mankind.

While the universal church and the individual churches may be distinguished, they are also related. The individual churches have no life apart from the life that they find in the universal church. The universal or spiritual church is not an institution, but is involved in the life of the world so that it might communicate the Word of God through the Christian community of faith to a world in need of God's truth and life.

The churches as organized societies of humans have always been tainted with imperfections. We can see this very clearly as we study the history of the churches. We read in the Bible that Jesus ordained the church and anointed it with the Holy Spirit on the day of Pentecost. We read how the church grew under the leadership of the Holy Spirit and the disciples of Christ. Also, as we read the Epistles in the Bible we see the work of the Holy Spirit and the Apostles establishing new churches and spreading the gospel and the message of Jesus Christ throughout Europe and the East.

For three hundred years after Christ's death, Christians had lived in danger of mob violence and toward the end of this period mob action and local persecution had been replaced by a concerted effort to destroy the Christian movement as a whole. Then with dramatic suddenness, the persecuted position of the Christian communities within the Roman Empire was brought to an end. Almost overnight Christianity emerged from its status as an illegal faith into the role of being the favored and then the official religion of the emperor Constantine.

Other Roman emperors had thought they could make the empire strong by destroying the Christian communities. Constantine, finding himself in a difficult situation, tried the opposite policy. He thought that if he could not destroy the Christians, he would join them.

He decided that his position might be strengthened by the Christian God in his service. The gamble paid off. His opponents were defeated. In anticipation of further benefits to be derived from the Christian god, Constantine took the church under his protection, showered it with favors and assumed responsibility for its affairs.

The struggle between the church and the state for power led to corruption in the church and it was not until the Protestant Reformation led by Martin Luther that the practices and teachings of the church were brought back to the Scriptures.

After the Protestant churches were organized, many of these groups continued to have the church and state connected. Then many Christians, who were seeking religious freedom, came to America where our constitution and by-laws guarantee men and women the freedom to worship God as they feel led.

Today we live in a day and age when God is at work all around us and we need to look for His call to join Him. We as individual Christians and as a church should be open to God's leadership. As we have looked very briefly at the history of Christ's church, we can see who we are. We are God's people.

If Christ is to build a better world through His church, we must know what we stand for. The church is challenged to be relevant to the needs of our day and at the same time fulfill God's purpose of keeping and proclaiming the gospel of Jesus Christ.

Baptists have a unique message and I believe that God has blessed Baptists in many ways because of their emphasis upon the scriptures, their missionary activities, and their evangelistic message. Let me very briefly point out to you six major Baptist doctrines, or Biblical doctrines, that I feel our churches must keep and proclaim in the world.

First, we believe the Bible teaches the priesthood of the believer. This means that every Christian has a direct access to God through faith in Jesus Christ. Also, that a sinner receives forgiveness by confessing his sins directly to God as revealed through Jesus Christ in His Word. It also means that all Christians are priests under God, both lay men and lay women, with the charge to minister to all those who have needs.

Second, we believe the scriptures are the source of our faith and life, for "*all scripture is given by inspiration of God and is profitable for doctrine, for reproof, for correction, for instruction in righteousness*" (2 Timothy 3:16).

Third is the principle of separation of church and state. Jesus said, "*Then render unto Caesar the things that are Caesar's and unto God the things that are God's*" Matthew 22:21. The church should not be over the state and the state should not be over the church. We need a free church in a free society.

Fourth, Baptist churches are governed by their independent local congregationals with each member having one vote.

Fifth, salvation is by faith in Christ through the grace of God, not of works, lest any man should boast. It is the gift of God. (Ephesians 2:8-9)

Sixth, Baptists have two church ordinances, one of baptism and the other is the Lord's Supper. Baptism symbolizes the death, burial and resurrection of Christ, showing that we should live in the newness of life. Baptism symbolizes immersion in obedience to Christ's command. The Lord's Supper includes the bread representing Christ's body that was given for us and the fruit of the vine symbolizing Christ's blood that was shed for the remission of our sins.

Now that we see <u>who we are</u> and what we stand for, we need to think about where God wants us to go. God wants us to <u>provide a place of divine worship to glorify Christ</u>. Worship is a person reaching up and out to God and God reaching down and within an individual. Worship helps in the renewal of faith and gives one a vision of God's Kingdom. Worship gives God a chance to give insight into what is right and wrong. Worship should bring confession for all have sinned and come short of the glory of God. As Isaiah said, "*Woe is me, for I am undone, because I am a man of unclean lips. For my eyes have seen the king, the Lord of hosts*" Isaiah 6: 5.

In a worship experience you may hear the voice of the Lord saying, "*Whom shall I send and who will go for us?*" And you may want to say with Isaiah, "*Here am I, Lord, send me.*" Evangelism is the word that tells us how Christ's church can build a better world. Its voice increases in volume as new converts become loudspeakers for Christ. Another place that God would have us to go is to every individual person who needs to accept Christ as their Savior. Never did people need more desperately what the church has to offer in terms of the gospel's creative, redemptive love and sustaining fellowship with God. How sad it is that many people go on week after week with fear and discouragement when faith in Jesus could give them a new life of peace, hope and love.

Christ commanded His Church to build a better world when He said,

> "*Go ye therefore and make disciples of all nations, baptizing them in the name of the Father and of the Son and of the Holy Spirit. Teaching them to observe all things and lo, I am with you always, even to the end of the world*" Matthew 28: 18-20.

The message of Christ must be heard, its influence felt, and its teachings practiced. The church can never rise above the level of its leadership. We must begin with Christians and their dedication to the Lord.

INTRODUCING THE MESSIAH TO YOUR FRIENDS

How do you witness to another student? The last recorded words of our Lord before His ascension are an encouragement to witness.

> "*But you shall receive power, after that the Holy Ghost is come upon you: and you shall be witnesses unto me both in Jerusalem, and in all Judea, and in Samaria, and unto the uttermost part of the earth.*" Acts 1:8

A witness is one who shares his own experience of what Christ has done in his life. A student who has had a life-changing experience has something to share. The strongest case for Christianity is the testimony of a changed life. The Holy Spirit uses the witness of God's word and the testimony of Christians to open the eyes of the lost to their personal need. Everyone has a realm of influence. It relates to families, friends, neighbors, and business associates. Each Christian is strategically placed so that everyone will have the opportunity to know Jesus Christ as Lord and Savior.

Here are the three steps to writing out your own personal testimony. First, tell about your life before you became a Christian, your life style, your relationship to the church, and the Bible. Second, tell about how the Lord revealed Himself to you and how you responded to Jesus' convicting spirit. Third, tell about your life-style now and what a difference Christ has made in your life.

How do you answer those who have questions when you are witnessing?

Challenge: I don't need to go to church; I am just as spiritual, if not more so, than those that go to church. I will worship God my way.

Response:

- Going to church is much more than only worship. It also involves growth through learning and fellowship with fellow student seekers.
- If you are strong in the faith, the church needs you to help others. If you are not strong in the Christian faith, you need Christ and the church to help you.
- Let me encourage you to make the church central to your life. Part of worshipping God is obeying Him, and God has clearly stated that

we are not to forsake our gathering together as a body of believers.

Questions for the skeptic:

- Can you honestly say that you have grown in the Christian faith "worshipping your way"?
- Don't you think there is the danger of spiritual, backsliding, which is usually the result of being on your own?

Challenge: How can you be so sure of an afterlife, and if there is an afterlife, how can a God of love condemn someone to Hell?

Response:

- God doesn't condemn any one to Hell. We condemn ourselves. (John 3:16-17)
- Heaven is provided by God as a final abode for the believer. The alternative is Hell for the unbeliever.
- Hell is the place for those that don't desire to go to heaven God's way. God's way is through faith in Christ, not through good works or being a decent person.
- Belief in Christ not only provides eternal benefits, but also practical benefits in this life. (John 10: 9-19) Example: One is more likely to live longer and healthier life, and likely to have

a happier marriage . . . and likely to contribute to your fellow man and woman.

- The Holiness and Righteousness of God's sense of justice demands consequences for disobedience; it demands a judgment. The product of that judgment may be exclusion from Heaven, or what is equivalent is going to Hell. Our selfish desires impel us to do it "our way" and our way is not God's way. God's way is through Christ. The very basis of Christianity is that none of us need go to Hell. A genuine belief in Christ is God's solution so you can go to Heaven rather than to Hell.
- Since God is perfection, we must be totally righteous in His presence, and that can only be achieved through Christ. If we reject Christ, we are reserving a place for ourselves in Hell. Christ clearly teaches the existence of an afterlife and the coming Judgment. (John 14: 2-3)

Questions for the skeptic:

- Wouldn't a God of Love create a Heaven, an eternal abode for his beloved children?
- Name one compelling reason impelling you to reject the existence of an afterlife?

Challenge: How about the people that never heard about Christ? How can God exclude them from Heaven?

Response:

- From the beginning God wanted his people to spread the knowledge of God's redemptive plan to all nations. The Great Commission in the Bible tells us to share the gospel throughout the world.
- The growth rate of Christianity has been astounding, for instance in South Korea, China and Nepal and even through the underground churches, which are prohibited by law. The internet is also available for further information around the world.

Questions for the unbeliever:

- Now that you have heard the gospel, you have no excuse. What will you do with Jesus?

Challenge: Even if there is a Heaven, what makes you think Christianity is the only way to get there?

Response:

- Christ is the only one who came from heaven and lived a perfect life. Then he died for our sins and rose from the grave and He has gone back to heaven to prepare a place for everyone who will receive Him as their Savior. More than 200 prophesies in the old Testament came true concerning Christ's life, purpose, death and resurrection.

Challenge: How can you be so sure there is a God?

Response:

- God created the world we live in, and He reveals Himself in nature.
- God is a person and He reveals Himself to those who believe by faith.
- God has changed my life and He lives in my heart. That is how I know there is a God.

Questions for the unbeliever:

- Have you asked Jesus to reveal Himself to you?
- Have you read the Bible that tells you about God?

Challenge: I can't trust the Bible, it is full of contradictions.

Response:

- The Bible is the Word of God with no contradictions.
- If you were a Christian, the Holy Spirit would help you to understand the scriptures so you could see there are no contradictions.

Questions for the unbeliever:

Do you accept and believe the parts of the Bible that are true?

Challenge: Do you really believe in a virgin birth?

Response:

- Yes, Jesus's virgin birth was prophesied 700 years earlier. This was the way Jesus was born so He would not inherit a sinful nature from Adam.

Challenge: I am not ready . . . I am not good enough.

Response:

- You will never be good enough until you accept Jesus Christ as your Savior. Come just as you are and accept Christ and He will make you a new person.

WHEN REJECTED, TURN TO JESUS

This lesson describes the challenges to Jesus' mission during his ministry: His home town rejected Him, His disciples feared Him, and the religious establishment distrusted Him. This lesson can help you overcome the inevitable challenges of following Jesus. I want to talk to those who had their purses stolen, and to those whose family members are not Christians. Do you feel rejected?

I grew up in a family of veterinarians. My father was a professor of veterinary science at Auburn University in Alabama. My two brothers, my brother—in—law, my uncle and my cousin were all veterinarians and I felt like a black sheep in the family. My daddy offered to send me to vet school, but I told him the Lord was calling me into full-time Christian service.

In 1996, my first wife of 50 years died of cancer and I felt all alone. Then in 1998 God led me to a wonderful Christian lady who plays the piano and sings to the glory of God. When you have your purse stolen, you feel rejected by the world! Who can you trust? This must have been the way Jesus felt when he went back to his home town to preach to his own people and they rejected him. The Gospel of Mark tells us about Jesus when he went to his home town.

> *"And he went out from thence, and came into his own country; and his disciples followed him. And when the Sabbath day was come, he began to teach in the synagogue; and many hearing him were astonished, saying, "from whence hath this man these things? And what wisdom is this which is given unto Him, that even such mighty works are wrought by his hands? Is not this the carpenter, the son of Mary, the brother of James, and Joses, and Judah, and Simon? And are not his sisters here with us? And they were offended at Him. But Jesus said unto them, 'A Prophet is not without honor, but in his own country, and among his own kin, and in his own house.' And He could there do no mighty work, save that He laid his hands upon a few sick folk, and healed them. And he marveled because of their unbelief and he went round about the villages teaching." Mark 6:1-6*

Jesus had been working at Capernaum and at other places in Galilee. He came to Nazareth, his home town. He went into the synagogue in Nazareth, where He had grown up. He probably had attended synagogue school there. He certainly had the custom of worshiping there on each Sabbath day.

Jesus had his disciples with him, and the synagogue leaders asked him to teach and the people were astonished because of the wisdom of His teaching and the power of the mighty works of healing. They began to ask questions that became increasingly hostile: "Is not this the carpenter, the son of Mary?" The people began to question Jesus' words because they could not get past His humble beginnings.

The failure of Mark to mention Joseph implies that Joseph was dead. Mark listed Jesus' brothers by name and the words reveal that Jesus also had sisters. Thus Mary had at least seven children but his brothers did not believe in Jesus as the Messiah until after the resurrection. The risen Lord appeared to His brother James. Later James became the leader of the Jerusalem church and he wrote the Book of James in the Bible. Jesus' brother Jude wrote the letter bearing his name.

Many believers who have family members who are unbelievers realize that Jesus can identify with them—Jesus also had unbelieving family members. You can also take heart because His brothers eventually became believers. Just keep praying for them. God answers prayers.

The result of the people's rejection was that Jesus was not able to do any miracles there, except that He laid His hands on a few sick people and healed them. This passage is an amazing picture of some of the concessions that Jesus placed upon Himself. Obviously, Christ as God could have done anything, but Jesus did not do many miracles because He limited Himself according to people's responses.

When we face rejection, we must put it in perspective. We may have felt let down by those who rejected us. So was Jesus, but we cannot take it personally. As it must have saddened Jesus' heart to see the rejection of His own hometown, we also should be saddened by those who reject the presence of Christ in us.

JESUS TELLS US HOW TO OVERCOME FEAR

Immediately after feeding the 5000, Jesus constrained his disciples to get into the ship and head across the Sea of Galilee. Jesus wanted time to pray. After the feeding miracle, there was a movement to take Jesus by force "to make Him king." Apparently the disciples were with the crowd and Jesus wanted to get them away from having any part in this plot. Jesus had tried to lead them to understand that He had not come to be an earthly king. After sending away the disciples, Jesus departed into a mountain to pray. When evening came, the boat was in the middle of the sea, and He was alone on the land. Jesus was able to see their plight. Jesus "*saw them toiling in rowing, for the wind was contrary unto them and about the fourth watch of the night he cometh unto them, walking on the sea, and would have passed by them. But when they saw him, walking upon the sea, they supposed it had been a spirit, or a ghost and they cried out: For they all saw him, and were troubled. And Jesus said unto them, "Be of good cheer: it is I: be not afraid*" (Mark 6:48 – 50). And he went up unto them into the ship and the wind ceased and they were "sore amazed" in themselves beyond measure, and wondered. We need to remember that each Christian experiences some storms in life, and Jesus knows and cares about us. Sometimes Jesus delivers us from a storm and sometimes through the storm. We need to be like Peter and step out in faith, but keep our eyes on Jesus.

GOD WANTS TO BLESS YOU

When I was 15 years old I accepted Jesus Christ as my Savior, and for 75 years He has been blessing me and I want to share with you how God wants to bless you. God wants to bless you spiritually and financially if you will join in a covenant relationship with Him. Spiritually, God says in His word that, "*If you will confess with your mouth that Jesus is Lord and you will believe in your heart that God has raised Him from the dead you will be saved*" (Romans 10: 9-10) and you will receive eternal life forever. That is His first blessing that he wants to give you.

The financial blessing is shown in God's word when it says if you will bring the whole tithe into the storehouse of God (the church) then God will throw open the floodgates of heaven and pour out so many blessings that you will have more than enough for your every need (Malachi 3:10). The storehouse of God is His church, and the tithe is 10% of what we earn or receive. You cannot out-give God, because God loves a cheerful giver.

God loves you, so why do many not give anything? Why rob God? God has made it possible for you to earn 100% of what you have, so 10% belongs to God if you want His blessings. Ninety percent will go further and buy more with God's blessings than one hundred percent will buy without God's blessings. Some of you only give a tip now and then to the church. You give a bigger tip to the waitress when you eat out. Sometimes you give 15% or 18%, or even 20% for really good service. Why don't you give 10% back to God when He makes it possible for you to earn 100%? Why are you missing all the blessings that God wants to give you?

> "*Prove me now herewith saith the Lord of hosts, if I will not open you the windows of heaven, and pour you out a blessing, that there shall not be room enough to receive it*" Malachi 3:10.

Roy and Ruth Isbell (1998-

TESTIMONY OF ROY S. ISBELL, SR.

Let me share with you what the Lord Jesus Christ has been doing in my life since I became a Christian, seventy—five years ago. I am now 91 years young and I still play tennis five days a week. In 1919, right after the First World War was over, I was born into a wonderful Christian family in Startown, North Carolina (now called Newton, N.C.). My mother and daddy were wonderful Christians and they taught me what was right and what was wrong and I thought I was a good boy, but that did not make me a Christian. When I was 15 years, old my mother took my younger brother and sister and me to a revival meeting in an empty furniture store in Auburn, Alabama.

That night the preacher told me how much God loved me and how He died for me on the cross for my sins, and that I needed to repent of my sins. I realized I was having sinful thoughts, and selfish thoughts. I was telling lies and then I would have to tell another lie to get out of telling the first lie. That night I received Jesus Christ into my life as my Lord and Savior, and I started growing in Christ. At this time we were living in the middle of the great depression of 1932-38. My daddy was a professor of veterinary medicine at Auburn University, but the state could not pay professors with money—only with IOU statements. The food store would accept the IOUs for us to buy food. For money, Daddy would milk cows at a dairy for 10 cents an hour before he would go to the university to teach.

I got my first job delivering newspapers on a route for 75 cents a week. A few years later I had my own newspaper delivery agency and sold the Sunday paper at a newsstand, but when it was time to go to Sunday School and church, I would close the newsstand and go to Sunday School and church until church was over.

My Mother, Addie McMahan Isbell

My brothersand sisters, My Father, Step Mother and Aunt

When I went to college I wanted to make a lot of money, so I majored in business administration, but God showed me that I needed to be more like some other college students who were fully dedicated to Jesus. I saw that they had a spiritual witness and a deeper commitment with Christ and that was something I wanted in my life. I started praying, and studying the Bible with them. As my relationship with Christ grew and my stewardship of money and time changed, my goal in life changed also. My new philosophy of life was found in Matthew 6:33. "But *seek ye first the Kingdom of God and His righteousness, and then all these things shall be added unto you.*" This scripture verse became my way of life.

In 1938-39 I took ROTC in college and also took flying lessons and learned to fly a Piper Cub plane. In 1941 our country went to war to stop Hitler and the Japanese from their evil acts around the world.

Even though I felt God calling me to serve Him as a college campus minister, I also felt like I should do my part in the war effort and then I would prepare myself to follow Christ's call to be a college campus minister.

In 1942 I joined the Navy Air Corp. and I was stationed at the University of South Carolina in Columbia, South Carolina for three months learning to identify all the German planes and ships in 100th of a second as they were flashed on a screen. We took many classes in Navy rules and drills. We then went to the University of Georgia in Athens, Georgia for three months where we studied Morse code until we could receive and send 12 words per minute. We then went to Olatha, Kansas where we started flying Waco and Steermans. We would start landing them in a large circle so we would be able to land on an aircraft carrier. After three months, they said they had 10,000 too many pilots in training, so I joined the Merchant Marine Academy.

As a cadet Midshipman, I went to sea on a tanker transporting gasoline for the airplanes in England. We would join about sixty other ships and go over in a convoy dodging the German submarines. One morning when I went on duty, they told me that during the night a German submarine had sunk a tanker ship just behind our ship.

On our last trip to London Bay in England they ordered our ship to stay in the bay because the bay was full of ships loaded with men ready for the "D" Day invasion. After the invasion started we returned to New York City and Texas where we loaded up with oil to take to our Navy ships in the South Pacific. We went through the Panama Canal and unloaded at Yap Island in the South Pacific.

From there we came back to the Academy in Great Neck Long Island, NY to finish our training. A few months later the war was over and I asked them to discharge me so I could go to the seminary and prepare for the ministry. There were many times during the war that I know God was protecting me for Him to use me in His ministry. One time I remember when we were in the English Channel going north near Norway and the fog was so thick you could not see the front of the ship. I was steering the ship keeping it on compass heading with the Captain nearby when the watchman on the bow of the ship called out, "Ship ahead broadside!" The captain grabbed the wheel and spun it all the way to the right and at the same time he cut the steam off completely. We barely missed the other ship.

In 1945 I enrolled in the Southern Baptist Seminary in Louisville, Kentucky and it was like a touch of heaven as I studied under some of the greatest Christian teachers in that generation. That summer I went back to Auburn University to finish my college work and I met my future wife while we were serving in the Baptist Student Union at Auburn University.

There were many young men returning from the war and going to college on the G.I. Bill, so we helped out in many youth revivals all over the South. We courted that summer and she was planning to graduate the next December. Before I left for the seminary in the fall I asked her to marry me when she graduated in December and she agreed.

In December 1946, I was ordained to the ministry on a Sunday. On Monday, my wife-to-be, Lou Warren, graduated from Auburn University at 3:00 p.m. We were married at 5:00 p.m. so she could return with me and enroll in the seminary also. I pastored the Hope Rescue Mission of Walnut Street Baptist Church in downtown Louisville, Kentucky until I graduated from the seminary.

In 1950-51, the Lord called me to serve Him and some wonderful college students at Delta State University in Cleveland, Mississippi. On a salary of $200 a month and with some supply preaching, we bought a house on the "GI bill" and we had our first baby, R. Sherman Isbell, who is now pastor of a church in Washington, D. C.

In 1953, our daughter was born and she is now Dr. Sally Isbell Powers, professor of psychology at the University of Massachusetts Amherst after getting her doctor's degree from Harvard University. She is also the mother of my two grandchildren: Sophia Powers completed her master's degree at Columbia University and is getting her Ph.D. at UCLA, and Max Powers is attending his third year at Vassar College.

From 1951-60, the Lord called me to serve as the Baptist Campus Minister at Mississippi State University where the Lord blessed the BSU Ministry to grow from one small office room in the YMCA on the campus to a full program. This included a Baptist Student Union Executive Student Council made up of a **President**, in charge of programs and leadership; **V.P.** in charge of enlistment and evangelism; a **Devotional Chairman** in charge of promoting prayer-mates, and dorm Bible studies; a M-F noon-day devotion time for 15 minutes; a **BSU Choir director** in charge of a 35-voice choir, their weekly choir practice, and two state-wide choir trips to three or four different Baptist churches each year; **a Social director** to plan and direct socials, banquets, and recreational activities for the BSU; a **Transportation director** in charge of drivers and a large bus to take students to church, BSU choir trips, and to Ridgecrest, a Baptist Assembly for student week each year in North Carolina. Each Council Member had at least five students under him to help him carry out his duties to God.

This made up the BSU Greater Council with at least one freshman on each committee. We also had a Married Student council with a monthly covered dish meal with an outstanding speaker to help married students and their spouses understand the joy of living under Jesus' leadership. We had a Baptist faculty group that met together to discuss a book or a Baptist doctrine each month, or quarter. We also had an international student banquet once a year for all the International Students on the campus with the University President bringing the Christian spiritual message.

We bought 12 acres of land next to the campus to build a Baptist Student Center. That center has served to reach over 350 college students each year for the last 50 years and now they are planning to build a four million dollar Baptist Student Center to reach even more students for Christ.

The Baptist Student Union is a movement and a spirit that is contagious when you are with a group of Christian students who love the Lord. They sing together, work together, and witness together in everyday living. Most campuses have a BSU Center that is used as a meeting place for fellowship, worship, discussion groups, Bible study and leadership training so students can go out to be witnesses for Christ on the campus. The BSU is an arm of all the Southern Baptist churches in a state seeking to minister to all the college students on all campuses in that state.

In 1960, I went to Southwestern Baptist Seminary to get a master's degree in Religious Education. At this time I chose another verse of scripture to live by, and it is:

> *"I beseech you therefore, brethren, by the mercies of God, that you present your bodies a living sacrifice, holy, acceptable unto God, which is your reasonable service. And be not conformed to this world: but be you transformed by the renewing of your mind, that you may prove what is that good, and acceptable, and perfect will of God."* **Romans 12: 1-2**

After I graduated, the Lord called me to serve as Campus Minister at the University of Missouri in Columbia, Missouri. I served there for ten years, also serving as a Volunteer Associate Statewide BSU Director. I then went to be the Associate Pastor of the First Baptist Church in Columbia, Missouri for four years. Next, I was called to start a new church in Midway Heights Community just out of Columbia, Missouri. To raise money for this new church I did real estate work until we built the new church building and called a full-time pastor. My wife was a professor in child development at the University of Missouri. Ten years before we retired we decided to buy a rental house each year and rent them out for our retirement days. We did this for seven years.

In 1982, we retired and started doing volunteer mission work with the Home Mission Board. We bought an Air Stream motor home to do mission work in Colorado, Massachusetts, in Florida at Miami University, in Orlando at Florida Central University, and Florida Atlantic University in Boca Raton, Florida. In 1993, we built a house in Boca Raton where we found the wonderful Boca Glades Baptist Church with a great Bible-preaching pastor, Pastor Truman Herring, where I now serve as a volunteer staff member. When the church voted to build the Family Life Center, Pastor Truman asked me to be chairman of the building committee. I suggested to Truman that we ask Keith Emery to be Co-chairman in charge of building and I would be co-chairman in charge of committees and raising money. Many said we could not do it. We organized the committees and had many discipleship courses taught. Most of the ones who took the course on **Experiencing God**, said, "Yes, we can do it, with God's help." By the time the Family Life Center was completed, the money was pledged and the building was paid for.

When the church voted to build a new sanctuary and office building, Pastor Truman asked me to be Chairman of the Building Committee. Again I asked Truman to ask Keith Emery to be the co-chairman in charge of building. With a lot of praying many church members worked hard to make our prayers come true. Pastor Truman and the Lord moved a mountain of dirt, and raised more money, and prayed over every decision until it was completed to be more than we dreamed it would be.

In 1996, my first wife Lou died of cancer after fifty years of a beautiful marriage. She was a professor at the University of Missouri and one of the national leaders in the Head Start Program under President Johnson. Our first child was a boy and he is a pastor in Washington D.C. My younger brother's (who was converted on the same night I was) first son is an ordained pastor in Birmingham, Alabama to a converted Jewish group. Also my younger sister's (who was also converted that same night) first son became a pastor of one of the largest churches in Birmingham, Alabama, Shades Mountain Baptist Church.

Pastor Truman's vision of missions in India inspired me to go to India in 2006, 2007, and 2008 to preach to thousands and many of them made decisions for Christ.

In 1998 I married Ruth Jones of Birmingham, Alabama. She is a wonderful Christian, and I love to hear her play the piano and sing. We now live the winter months in Boca Raton, Florida and the summer months in Birmingham, Alabama. My hobbies are playing tennis and chess. My most important time of the day is my quiet time of Bible study with the Lord each morning.

When we are in Birmingham, Alabama in the summer months, we attend South Roebuck Baptist Church where we are choir members and do extra jobs like changing the messages on the church sign each week, and teaching the senior adult Sunday School class when they need us.

In the last four years, this church has started a new 30 acre campus with a building to care for over 100 children and a program that reaches around 600. There is one church with two campuses in a fast growing community. God is very good and, the Lord willing, I hope to be serving Him until I am 105+.

MY YOUNGER BROTHER IS TRULY A MAN OF GOD

Dr. W. J. Isbell, Jr. graduated in Veterinary Medicine from Auburn University and practiced until the Lord called him into full-time Christian work. He served as State Brotherhood Director for the Alabama Baptist Convention. From there the Lord called him to serve as Baptist Men's Director with the Southern Baptist Convention, and later to serve as the Baptist Men's Brotherhood Director for the Texas Baptist Convention. After retirement he served as the Director of Baptist Men for the Baptist World Alliance.

W. J. is one year and eleven months younger than I am. Our mother would dress us alike. When I started school in the first grade they let my younger brother go to school with me. (Maybe it was because our daddy was Teacher of Agriculture and the basketball coach at that school.) We both made all A's, but they would not let him go on to the second grade because he was too young. I will always be grateful for the relationship and spiritual inspiration that I have had with him for his 89 years.

BAPTIST STUDENT DIRECTORS WHO HAVE BLESSED MY LIFE

(And the Lives of Thousands of Other Students)

Dr. Frank Leavell	The first Southern Baptist Convention Director of Student Work

In 1939, my younger brother, Dr. W. J. Isbell, Jr., went to one of the first South-wide Student Conferences in Memphis, Tennessee.

Dr. Kerne Keene	The second Southern Baptist Convention Director of Student Work
Dr. David Alexander	The third Southern Baptist Convention Director of Student Work
Dr. Bob Denney	Southern Baptist Convention Assistant Director

I invited Bob Denny to speak to our students at a Religious Emphasis week at Delta State University in 1950.

Dr. William Hall Preston	Southern Baptist Convention Assistant Director
Art Driscole	Southern Baptist Convention Assistant Director
Nell Magee	Southern Baptist Convention Assistant Director
Ed Seabaugh	Southern Baptist Convention Assistant Director
Ed Rollins	Southern Baptist Convention Assistant Director
Miss Mom Green (Potts)	1938-1939 Auburn University
Mr. T. C. Clark 1940-41	Auburn University BSU Director

We both signed up to serve in the Navy at the same time in 1941.

Charles Roselle	Auburn University and University of Missouri

	Southern Baptist Convention Director of Student Work
Jamie Jones	University of Arkansas BSU Director
Harold Gulley	Auburn University BSU Director
Dot Lee Merrill	Delta State University, Cleveland Mississippi
Jimmy Breland*	Delta State University, BSU Director
Bill Kirkpatrick	Delta State University, BSU Director
Charles Horner	State BSU Director of Mississippi
Joe Webb	State BSU Director of Florida
Frank Horton	Mississippi State University and Louisiana State University
Louie Farmer	Mississippi Southern University

In 1958 we carried 28 students to the Baptist World Alliance Youth Conference in Toronto, Canada in our Mississippi State BSU bus visiting Southern Baptist Convention places and seminaries on the way.

Marian Leavell	University of Mississippi
Katheryn Jasper	Mississippi College for Women
Betty Jean (Denny)	Mississippi College for Women
Ralph Winders	State BSU Director of Mississippi
Wayne Robbins*	Vice President of Belmont College in Tennessee
Jerry Merriman*	State BSU Director of Mississippi
Dr. Ernie Beevers*	State BSU Director of Ohio (MIT)
Elgin Lee	State BSU Director of Missouri

Bill Marshall	State BSU Director of Missouri
Charlie Johnson	State BSU Director of Missouri and Southern Baptist Convention
Dr. Fred Neiger	Bible Professor at University of Missouri
Charlie Johnson	Southern Baptist Convention Director of Student Work
Dr. Loy Reed	State BSU Director of Florida
Dr. W. F. Howard	State BSU Director of Texas
Byron Kirpatrick	University of Florida
Michael Ball	Mississippi State University
June Scoggins	Mississippi State University
Steve Thompson	Auburn University
Jerry Carmichael	University of Missouri

*One of my BSU students while I was the BSU Director.

BAPTIST STUDENT CENTERS WHERE I HAVE SERVED THE LORD

AUBURN UNIVERSITY (Auburn, Alabama) (1938-1940 and 1945-1949)

The First Baptist Church in Auburn, Alabama is where I was baptized and where I was married and preached a few times. As a BSU student, the Lord called me to be a campus minister. The Baptist Student Center is located at 135 North College Street, Auburn, Alabama.

DELTA STATE UNIVERSITY (Cleveland, Mississippi) (1950—1951)

The Baptist Student Center is located at 903 South Court Street, Cleveland, Mississippi.

Three BSU Director at Delta State University. Jimmy Breland, Roy Isbell, and Bill Kirkpatrick

MISSISSIPPI STATE UNIVERSITY (Starkville, Mississippi) (1951-1960)

The Baptist Student Center is located at 1169 East Lee Blvd., Starkville, Mississippi.

UNIVERSITY OF MISSOURI (Columbia, Missouri) (1961—1970)

The Mizzou Baptist Student Center is located at 812 Hitt Street, Columbia, Missouri.

Jerry Carmichael, Director of the University of Missouri Baptist Student Ministries.

UNIVERSITY OF MIAMI (Miami, Florida) (1990-Hurricane Andrew and working with international students)

The Baptist Student Center is located at 1200 Stanford Drive, Coral Gables, Florida.

UNIVERSITY OF CENTRAL FLORIDA (Orlando, Florida) (1991-1992)

Baptist Campus Ministry Center on West University; Brad Crawford, Baptist Campus Ministry Director

FLORIDA ATLANTIC UNIVERSITY (Boca Raton, Florida) (1995)

First Baptist Church of Boca Raton on 2350 N.W. 51 Street

THE INCOMPLETE BIOGRAPHY

"And there are also many other things which Jesus did, the which, if they should be written every one I suppose that even the world itself could not contain the books that should be written." John 21: 25

Have you ever finished reading a good book and felt that it was incomplete; you would like for the story to go on and on? This is how Andrew and some of the other disciples who were with the Apostle John at Ephesus felt when John finished writing the Book of John.

The Gospel of John was the last of the four Gospels to be written. The Gospels by Matthew, Mark and Luke had been already some years in existence, and had gained for themselves an established position as authoritative records of the life of Christ. But the story of Jesus as told by the first three disciples was not a complete biography. It was a mere sketch of the life of Christ. There were whole sections of the story of Jesus that the first three writers passed over in silence.

Nowhere, perhaps, was the incompleteness of the story of Christ, as told by Matthew and Mark and Luke, more clearly recognized and deeply felt than at Ephesus. The Christians at Ephesus had enjoyed the rare privilege of having John as their pastor.

The church at Ephesus had heard John tell of mighty works that Jesus did, and of wonderful discourses that he delivered, of which no mention was made in the existing Gospels. And now that John was getting old, they didn't want these precious recollections of Christ to perish with John's death, so they began to press him to commit them to writing, so that they might become the church's permanent possession.

The story is told of how John's fellow-disciples, Andrew among them, urgently pressed John to write. John said, "Fast with me then for three days, and let us tell one another any revelation which may be made to us, for or against the plan of writing." On the very first night it was revealed to Andrew that John should relate all in his own words, and that all should review his writing. So John undertook the task, and produced for us the fourth Gospel—the most sublime book in the world. How many of you have read the Gospel of John all the way through?

I can imagine with eager anticipation how the Christians at Ephesus looked forward to the publication of John's Gospel. I can imagine the delight and deepening interest Andrew and the other disciples had after reading it when it was finished.

The story of the marriage feast in Cana of Galilee, the story of Nicodemus, the story of the Samaritan woman at the well, the sermon of the Good Shepherd, the story of Lazarus, and those imperishable words spoken in the silence of the upper room, were all in it and were only recorded in John's account.

And yet when they came to the end of verse 23 of the last chapter, mingled with their thankfulness and delight, there was a shade of disappointment. There were things that Andrew and the others who had been disciples of Christ missed from the story.

So after testifying that what John said was beautiful and true; so far as it went, they added a little note to warn readers against supposing that it was a complete biography. "*This is not all,*" they said. "*There are also many other things which Jesus did.*"

Then they began to realize that not even the beloved Apostle John could put all of Jesus into a book. It would require a vast library of books to tell the story of the Savior's life. "There are many other things which Jesus did" is their comment on this Gospel in Verse 25. John recorded only samples of the kind of words Jesus used to speak, and the kind of deeds He used to do His works.

The **incompleteness** of John's account and the **inexhaustibleness** of the theme are the two facts set forth in the words of this text. All we shall ever know of Jesus' earthly life is contained in four small booklets of Matthew, Mark, Luke and John, and that does not make a hundred pages between them. Compare the Gospels with famous modern biographies, and you will realize how short the story of Jesus is. And yet, if there is one thing that we are becoming more and more conscious of every year, it is that the Gospel story is an inexhaustible theme!

What was it about Christ and his life here on earth that was so important? The theme of the Gospel is that **Christ did something unique in the cross and resurrection that makes possible our redemption**. There is no other way. This is what life and Christianity is all about. God's power and spirit for doing good comes through Christ's redemptive work in our lives.

Because the life of Christ is not confined to 30 years in Palestine, Jesus did not end his career on that cross. He died and rose again, and for 20 centuries now Jesus has been alive and at work in the world. There can be no complete biography of Jesus Christ because His is an unfinished life. You can only write a complete biography of a person whose work is done, and whose life is at an end. And that is why the complete story of Jesus Christ cannot be written. Jesus is not dead. He is alive forevermore. The most anyone can do is to bring the story up to date, and write, "To be continued" on the next page.

What else would you put in this biography?

In any complete biography of Jesus Christ you would have to write the story of the Christian Church. The church is the body of Christ—his hands, his feet, his lips. He is the soul, the life within the body. By the church Christ speaks, acts and works. "*Apart from me,*" He said Himself, "*You can do nothing*" (John 15:5, NIV).

The achievements and triumphs of the church are really the achievements and triumphs of Christ. Apostles, evangelists, missionaries, teachers, pastors, and church members—these are the ambassadors. The real worker all the time is Christ and in any complete biography the story of the church through the centuries must find a place. The first volume of church history ever written is the volume known to us as the book of Acts of the Apostles.

In the book of Acts, Luke tells what Jesus continued to do by means of his holy Apostles, especially Peter and Paul. But the subject is still the same. The Gospel was the "Life of Christ, Vol. I"; the book of Acts is the life of Christ, Vol. II. For in all the suffering, working, and conquest of the early church, Luke saw Jesus suffering, working, and conquering.

In a complete biography of Christ you must tell of Christian missions. Thousands of books on church history and Christian missions tell us of many men and women who played a large part, but behind them all I see one majestic figure working in all, and that is the person of Jesus Christ.

When I hear of all our church members who went to India and Brazil, I see Jesus at work in what we did, for it was Jesus who convicted many of their sins and saved them for eternal life. When I read of the triumphs won for the gospel by great preachers like John Knox of Scotland, John Wesley, George Whitfield, Charles Spurgeon, D. L. Moody, Billy Graham and our own Pastors Truman, Sandy and Scott, and Pastors Chris Crain, Michael Etheridge, and Richard Hitchcock plus all the BSU Directors named in this book, then I am reading of the triumphs of Jesus. And when you are inclined to go the second mile in sharing your time, food, flowers, (Brenda Jones and Steve Johnson), and your friendship, and love of God, be assured you are not alone—it is God working in you.

In a complete biography you must include the history of self-sacrifice by laymen and women under the spirit of Christ. Loring Brace, an American author, describes the growing humaneness of life since the coming of Christ. He shows how the position of women has been elevated, and children have become objects of tender and loving care: he shows how private war and dueling have been abolished. He shows how the chains have been removed from the slave: he shows how a humane spirit has crept into our laws, and how the course of the centuries has been marked by a growing care for the poor, the minority, the orphan, the unfortunate, and the lost. And the book in which he tells this wonderful story he entitles "The Doings of Christ."

For it is Jesus Christ who has filled men and women's hearts with the emotions of sympathy and love, which have sent them forth to engage in service. The story of John Howard and his tireless labor for prison reform is part of the story of Christ. The story of Florence Nightingale and her unwearied ministry to the sick and wounded is part of the story of Christ. The work of the choir members and Sunday School teachers, the deacon's ministry, and witnessing are all doings of Christ.

When we realize that the complete story must embrace the history of all these good works plus many more done in the name and spirit of Christ we have to agree with the disciples that if all the things that Jesus did were written down, the world itself could not contain the books that should be written.

The story of missions, and charity and self-sacrifice and the story of the church do not complete the biography of Christ. For each person would want the things Jesus had done for him or her included. We have each of us a chapter to supply for the biography of Christ, and until each believer has written down what the Lord has done for him, the account is still incomplete.

In conclusion, someday this life on earth will be complete. The Bible tells us about the "coming of the end," when Christ shall have delivered up the kingdom of God to the Father after the final Judgment. The history of Christ's redemptive work will then be complete, and you can write 'Finished' at the end. In that complete biography shall you find a place? To complete it, you must have chapters declaring what Christ has done for us. Or will it be complete without you and your loved ones? Our eternal destiny hangs on our answer to that question, for the complete biography is the Lamb's Book of Life. For only those **who believe in Christ** will have a part with Christ in Heaven for eternity.

THIS IS YOUR LIFE TO RUN THE RACE

HEBREWS 12:1-3, 14

Today is the first day of the rest of your life, and the coach of your life, Jesus Christ, has come to recruit you to join His team and play a very important position on His team (the Church). If you will trust Him and obey Him as your coach, He promises to bring out the best in you as you work with the team to have a winning season every year.

You will receive a scholarship of training, fellowship, joy, love, and peace, and when you graduate He promises you will be in the Hall of Fame as a witness to all those who come after you. If you are willing to sign a letter of intent you must agree to the following rules.

1. You must be born again by the spirit of God.
2. To play on God's team you must be enrolled in the universal Church.
3. You must be faithful, and seek to pursue righteousness and obedience with the coach's

> help. Training and instructions, study of the manual, and fellowship with the coach will be so helpful and inspiring that you will not want to miss a single day as you prepare for the game of your life.

Our main game will be the Super Bowl, the World Series, the Davis Cup and every position in the Olympics as you represent the Kingdom of God. Our opposition will be Satan and all his fallen angels. Our coach has won the victory every time He played against Satan, but you must do your part if you want to be on the winning team. Hebrews 12:1 tells us that we will be playing in the World Bowl and have a great cloud of witnesses both on earth and in heaven.

Our main goal is to lead others to trust Christ as their Savior. As we live each day let us imagine ourselves as athletes in a great amphitheater with tiers of seats rising all around us. The spectators in them are the faithful people of all past history. They are "A cloud of witnesses" who testify of the power of God. Their experiences are to be a testimony forever of what God can do. For the mighty hand that led them is extended to us for guidance. They were not perfect men and women. Quite the contrary. They are to be our encouragement, for they show the strength of God's transforming power in spite of human weakness and failure. So forgetting those things which are behind, let us all press on toward the mark of the high calling in Christ Jesus, our coach, our Lord and our Savior. Let this Year be the best year of your life as you live each day to point others to Christ.

CHRIST IS COMING AGAIN

Look at the past to understand the future. Look into the future by setting goals, having hope, planning and preparing for the future so that when these days come we will be ready. By understanding the past and planning for the future, one is able to live today and tomorrow with meaning, purpose and a full life of Christian joy, peace, hope, and love.

Watch with hope, patience, zeal and purity until Christ comes. Christ's resurrection proved that He had plucked the sting out of sin and that his death did undo what sin had done. Christ's return to earth will climax his first advent as his resurrection climaxed his death.

Look at the signs of His coming:

1. One sign is false leaders and false prophets.
2. There will be wars and rumors of wars.
3. A third sign is tribulation.
4. A great turning away from religion. I Tim 4: 1-3

5. Men shall be lovers of their own selves and lovers of pleasures more than lovers of God. 2 Tim. 3: 1-4
6. The sixth sign of Christ's coming is the <u>spread of the Gospel.</u>

How can we know the time?

1. The manner in which the Lord will return will be sudden, personal, and universal.
2. There will be three primary results of Christ's return.
   a. The believing dead shall be raised.
   b. The books will be balanced. 2 Cor. 5:10
   c. It will be a source of joy to some and an occasion of bitter sorrow to others.

YET, THE LORD DELAYS HIS COMING. So we need to <u>witness</u> to as many as we can before it is too late.

TO BUY A BOOK FOR YOURSELF OR A FRIEND

TO ORDER DIRECTLY FROM AUTHORHOUSE:

Call 888-519-5121, OR ORDER ONLINE,
http://www.authorhouse.com/Bookstore/BookHome.aspx

E-BOOK $9.99
PAPERBACK $10.00
HARDBACK $14.95

IN A RETAIL OR BOOKSTORE:

E-BOOK $9.99
PAPERBACK $12.00
HARDBACK $22.50

HOW TO CONTACT ROY ISBELL

FOR CAMPUS EVENTS OR SIGNINGS

ruthnroy@gmail.com
cell: 205-965-8965

April—Oct. 1st
205-833-8766

Oct. 3—April 1st
561-477-0032

www.ingramcontent.com/pod-product-compliance
Ingram Content Group UK Ltd.
Pitfield, Milton Keynes, MK11 3LW, UK
UKHW040601210726
13854UKWH00008B/1710

9 781463 419578